Ancient Forests

CIRCLE OF LIFE · CIRCLE OF LIFE · CIRCLE OF LIFE · CIRCLE OF LIFE · CIRCLE OF LIFE · CIRCLE OF LIFE

Ancient
Forests

Alexandra Siy

DILLON PRESS
New York

Maxwell Macmillan Canada
Toronto

Maxwell Macmillan International
New York Oxford Singapore Sydney

For my father

Acknowledgments

The author would like to thank the Native Forest Council for providing information and photographs. Also thanks to Rosa Wilson and Susan Myers of the National Park Service, Lavonda Walton of the U.S. Fish and Wildlife Service, and Jill Bauermeister and Bernie Yee of the U.S. Forest Service for their work in obtaining photographs. Appreciation also goes to Brian Wilder for providing pictures.

I would also like to thank Mary Lou Grinwis of the Elizabethtown, New York, library for her help in obtaining research materials.

And a very special "thank you" goes to my husband, Eric, who provided me with inspiration and support for this book, and all books, in the Circle of Life series.

Photographic Ackowledgments

The photographs are reproduced through the courtesy of the Library of Congress: Darius Kinsey; National Forest Service: Curt Given, Jim Hughes, Roy Murphy, Yuen-Gi Yee; Native Forest Council: Daniel Dancer; U.S. Fish and Wildlife Service: M.D. Spanel, Randy Wilk; Visuals Unlimited: Geroge Herben, Peter K. Ziminski; Steve Warble; and Brian Wilder.

Library of Congress Cataloging-in-Publication Data

Siy, Alexandra.
   Ancient forests / by Alexandra Siy.
      p. cm. — (A Circle of life book)
   Includes index.
      Summary: Describes the life cycles of Douglas Firs in the Pacific Northwest as they relate to ecological issues such as species diversity and air and water filtration.
   ISBN 0-87518-466-9
   1. Old growth forests—Northwest, Pacific—Juvenile literature. 2. Forest ecology—Northwest, Pacific—Juvenile literature. 3. Forest conservation—Northwest, Pacific—Juvenile literature. 4. Species diversity—Northwest, Pacific—Juvenile literature. [1. Old growth forest. 2. Forests and forestry. 3. Forest ecology. 4. Forest conservation. 5. Ecology.] I. Title. II. Series.
   QH104.5.N6S58 1991
   581.5' 2642' 09795—dc20   91-15422

Dillon Press
Macmillan Publishing Company
866 Third Avenue
New York, NY 10022

Maxwell Macmillan Canada, Inc.
1200 Eglinton Avenue East
Suite 200
Don Mills, Ontario M3C 3N1

Macmillan Publishing Company is part of the Maxwell Communication Group of Companies.
First edition

Printed in the United States of America
10   9   8   7   6   5   4   3   2   1

Contents

▼

CANADA

NORTH CASCADES
NATIONAL PARK

OLYMPIC
NATIONAL PARK

*OLYMPIC
MOUNTAINS*

MT. BAKER-SNOQUALMIE
NATIONAL FOREST

OLYMPIC
NATIONAL FOREST

WASHINGTON

*PACIFIC
OCEAN*

Seattle

MT. RAINIER
NATIONAL PARK

Olympia

Columbia

GIFFORD PINCHOT
NATIONAL FOREST

River

Portland

MT. HOOD
NATIONAL FOREST

SIUSLAW
NATIONAL
FOREST

C O A S T   R A N G E S

C A S C A D E S

WILLAMETTE
NATIONAL FOREST

OREGON

UMPQUA
NATIONAL FOREST

CRATER LAKE
NATIONAL PARK

N

SISKIYOU
NATIONAL
FOREST

ROGUE RIVER
NATIONAL FOREST

*SISKIYOU
MOUNTAINS*

KLAMATH
NATIONAL
FOREST

*KLAMATH
MOUNTAINS*

SHASTA-
TRINITY
NATIONAL FOREST

ANCIENT
FORESTS

SIX RIVERS
NATIONAL FOREST

CALIFORNIA

Ancient Forests

Facts

Location: The Westside is the name given to the western parts of the Pacific Northwest, which includes the states of Washington, Oregon, and the northern part of California.

Climate: The climate is mild and wet, with from 70 to 100 inches of rain every year. Most of the rain falls in the winter.

Geography: The Westside has several mountain ranges: the Olympic Mountains, the Cascade Mountains, the Siskiyou Mountains, the Klamath Mountains, and the Coast Ranges.

Natural Resources: The most common trees in Westside ancient forests are Douglas firs. The tallest one on record rose 385 feet above the forest floor, but most reach only 300 feet. Douglas firs can live for more than 1,000 years and are the most valuable timber trees in the world.

Human Way of Life: For the past 100 years, many people living in the Westside have earned their living from logging.

Global Importance: Ancient forests help filter air and water. They are home to plants and animals that live nowhere else on earth and are rich in species diversity.

Current Status: Less than 15 percent of the ancient forests that once covered the Westside remain today.

CHAPTER 1

The Conifers—
Kings of the Forest

▼

Ancient forests are old forests. And old forests are big forests. Can you imagine trees that stand as high as a twenty-five-story skyscraper, or fallen logs the size of giant tractor-trailer trucks?

The Oldest Living Things

Now try to imagine how old a tree can be. Most trees in the ancient forests began life about 500 years ago. That means they have been around since the time Christopher Columbus first sailed to the Americas.

In fact, the oldest trees living in the Westside popped out of their seeds 3,500 years ago!

Trees are the oldest living things in the world. But only some kinds of trees can live for many thousands of years. The biggest and oldest trees in the world live in North America in a place called the Westside. The

Compared to the huge trees of an ancient forest,
a human being appears quite small.

ANCIENT FORESTS

▼

Westside is the western part of the Pacific Northwest. The Pacific Northwest includes the states of Washington, Oregon, and the northern part of California.

One hundred years ago, ancient forests covered almost all of the Westside. Now ancient forests grow only in smaller areas that are owned by the United States government. These national forests and national parks are found mostly in the Olympic Mountains in Washington, the Cascade Mountains in Washington and Oregon, and in the mountains along the coast in Oregon and northern California.

The Westside has perfect weather for growing big old trees. The Pacific Ocean makes the air very wet. When the wind blows, heavy clouds are pushed into the mountains. There the clouds burst and drop all their rain onto the ancient forests. In the winter it rains almost every day, but in the summer it is very dry.

The kinds of trees that can survive the dry summer and use the rains of the winter are called **conifers**. Conifers are trees that make cones instead of flowers. Inside the cones are seeds that can grow into new trees. Conifers also have needles instead of leaves.

Heavy clouds from the Pacific Ocean bring moist air, rain, and snow to the mountains and forests of the Pacific Northwest.

Since the needles stay on the trees throughout the year, the trees are often called evergreens. People use them for Christmas trees because they are green in the winter.

During the time of the dinosaurs, the earth was covered with conifers. Some scientists think dinosaurs used their long necks for feeding high in the tops of these ancient evergreens. Now trees with flowers and leaves, such as maple trees and apple trees, are more

common throughout the world. The Westside is one of the last places on earth where mostly conifers grow.

Many different kinds of conifers grow in the Westside. Each kind is part of a separate group called a **species**. A species is a group of animals or plants that are alike. Members of a species look alike and behave in similar ways. They can breed or mate with each other to produce seeds, eggs, young, or babies.

For example, dogs, cats, and people all belong to different species. Plants are grouped into species, too. In fact, scientists think there could be more than 20 million different species on earth!

There are twenty-five species of conifers in the Westside. Each is different in some ways from all the others. The most common species of conifer, the Douglas fir, is the world's third tallest. For many years it has been cut down and made into lumber for houses and ships.

Another Westside conifer is the Sitka spruce. This tree grows best in wet forests. In the early days of flying, it was used to build airplanes because its wood is strong and light.

The western hemlock is a Westside tree that grows

A Douglas fir cone.

quickly in shady, wet forests. It is used mostly for making paper.

A Story of Succession

All of the different kinds of conifers growing together make an ancient forest. But ancient forests were young once. Every giant tree started its life as a tiny seed on the floor of the forest. As time passed, many small trees died. The ones that were able to live through fires, storms, diseases, and droughts are the giant old trees left standing today.

The way a forest grows from a young forest of small trees to an old forest of large trees is called **succession**. Succession means the changes that happen over time in a forest. For example, one species grows first, and then after many years another species takes its place. This happens for hundreds of years until the forest reaches the last stage of succession. In a forest, the last stage is called **old growth**. It can take more than one thousand years for a forest to become old growth.

Imagine that succession is like a long story. The following story about succession is one that possibly

Fire plays an important part in succession in an ancient forest.

could have happened in a Westside forest.

One thousand years ago on a hot summer night, lightning strikes a giant old conifer. Fire quickly spreads over its dry needles. Soon the fire is everywhere. Many trees in the forest are burning.

Vegetation may begin to return within one month after a forest fire.

By morning the fire is out. Many treetops are burned off. Now sunshine reaches the forest floor where yesterday there was only shade. In the sunny places plants start to grow. A few months later, the forest floor is green with tiny new trees. The fastest-growing trees have the best chance of surviving.

For ten years many kinds of trees grow. But the Douglas firs are the tallest. The other trees cannot get enough sunlight in the shade of the Douglas firs.

Now fifty years have passed, and most of the other smaller trees have died. The Douglas firs are still growing. Less and less sunlight shines through the thick treetops to the forest floor.

It has been 200 years since the fire. Many Douglas firs are still growing tall and strong. But some have been blown over by windstorms, and others have been killed by disease. These fallen trees leave spaces where sunshine can reach the forest floor. In the sunny places new trees can grow again. Species such as western hemlock and Sitka spruce grow quickly on top of the fallen and dead Douglas fir **logs**.

For another 800 years, the hemlocks and spruces grow. Many more Douglas firs die and fall. One thousand years after the fire, the forest has reached its final stage. The ancient Douglas firs and Sitka spruces stand 300 feet tall. Below them, western hemlocks reach 200 feet from the forest floor. The forest is an old-growth forest.

The forest lives in this stage for hundreds of years until another fire, storm, or flood kills the big trees. When this happens, succession starts again.

CHAPTER 2

Life in a Log

▼

Ancient forests are more than big old trees. Old-growth forests are filled with many kinds of living things. You can smell the life. The air is fresh and smells of wood and damp earth. You can hear the life, too. Birds call, and animals scamper through the trees and in and out of logs. But sometimes it is hard to see the life. At first all your eyes can do is stare at the trees—trees so tall, so grand, that words cannot describe them.

But look closely! High in the treetops live animals and birds. Some of them come out only at night. And in a dead log on the ground there is even more life. Only forests with many large logs can be old-growth forests. Logs are the life of the forest.

All giant trees will some day die. When a tree dies, it brings new life to the forest. For many more years a

In an old-growth forest, dead logs on the ground help create new life.

dead tree is an important part of a Westside ancient forest.

Fire, wind, ice, insects, volcanoes, floods, disease— these are some of the things that kill trees. And it does matter how a tree dies.

Houses Made of Sticks

Some trees die standing up. These dead trees are called **snags**. Snags are like tall chimneys because they are hollow inside. They give protection and shelter to many animals.

Bears make dens in the bottom of snags. Inside, smaller animals such as squirrels, bobcats, and birds build nests and dens. The tops of snags make great lookouts for owls and hawks.

When a Douglas fir, or any other tree, dies and falls to the ground, it is called a log. Like snags, logs are made of dead wood. Dead wood is a soft wood because it is starting to rot, or **decompose**. When a tree decomposes, its wood is broken into small pieces. After a long time, the small, soft pieces of rotting wood get worked into the ground as part of the soil.

It can take hundreds of years for a Douglas fir log

This family of owls makes its home in the top of a snag.

to decompose completely. During this time the log provides many **habitats** for living animals and plants. A habitat is the place where a plant or animal lives. Each habitat has everything living things need for life—food, water, shelter, and protection from danger.

The forest is the habitat for many plants and animals. Each species needs different parts of the forest for life. What is important for the life of one animal may not be needed at all for another kind of animal.

For this reason, the forest is not just one habitat. It is thousands of habitats, because thousands of different species live in it.

The Bark Eaters

Just like a forest, the Douglas fir log provides many habitats for many different plants and animals. The first species to invade the log is the bark beetle. Bark beetles are insects that eat their way into the log. Once inside, they chew at the wood, making mazes and tunnels. Most bark beetles carry **spores** inside their bodies. Spores are tiny cells that can grow into **fungi**.

At one time fungi were thought to be plants. Now scientists know they are very different from plants. One difference is that they are not green, like plants. Plants can make their own food, but fungi cannot. Instead, they feed off of dead plants and animals. For this reason, they are also called **decomposers**.

Mushrooms and molds are fungi. Many other species live in different habitats all over the world. Some grow best on old bread or fruit. Others can grow on the tiny dead remains of bacteria buried in the ice at the North Pole.

A western hemlock tree grows on top of a fallen "nurse log" on the floor of an ancient forest.

The first fungi to invade the Douglas fir log feed on its inner bark. They grow quickly because there is so much wood on which to feed. More fungi means more beetles, because bark beetles eat fungi. The beetles make more and more openings and tunnels. Insects, spiders, snails, and salamanders creep and crawl through the tunnels. The log is habitat to all.

There's No Place Like Home

The log provides a habitat for plants, too. The roots of tiny trees take hold in the soft, rotting log. Since the

Big logs sometimes fall across rushing streams in old-growth forests.

log is always wet, like a sponge, young hemlocks and spruce have plenty of water. Decomposing logs are also filled with the **nutrients** young trees need for growth. Nutrients are the parts of food that help living things grow.

Without logs, most trees would not survive their first year of life. When a log finally decomposes completely, its remains go into the ground and make the soil healthier. The roots of the trees that began life on the log will use this soil for hundreds of years. Some day those trees will die and become logs, too.

As time goes on, more and more species depend on the log for life. Woodpeckers drill deep into the log for insects. Chipmunks, mice, and voles hide inside and under logs. There they are safe from snakes, foxes, and hawks.

Big logs sometimes fall across streams and make quiet pools. Here fish, frogs, insects, and salamanders can swim safely during heavy rains when streams are filled with rushing water.

Snags and logs help make a forest an old-growth forest. When trees in a Westside ancient forest are cut down and taken away, the habitat is also taken away. Without the big old trees, there are no snags or logs. Without snags and logs, there are fewer habitats. And without their habitats, plants and animals cannot survive. The forest becomes an empty place.

CHAPTER 3

The Ancient Ark

▼

Do you know the story in the Bible about Noah and his ark? Noah knew it would rain for forty days. He knew animals and plants could not survive if the land were covered with water. So Noah decided to save the living creatures of the earth by putting them in an ark that would float safely on the water. Noah's ark carried two of every animal—a male and a female. When the earth dried out, those animals went back to living on the land. They had babies, and life continued on earth.

In some ways ancient forests are like Noah's ark. The ark was a home to the animals, just as old-growth forests are home to many species. Like the ark, ancient forests **preserve** the life of species. When a plant or animal is preserved, it is protected from danger and has the habitat it needs for survival.

A saw-whet owl looks out from its home in an old-growth tree.

Ancient forests also preserve the future of species. All plants and animals must **reproduce** so that the species will live on into the future. Reproduction is the way plants and animals make seeds, eggs, babies, or young. Some animals and plants reproduce by mating or breeding. However, species can mate only if there is enough habitat for growing or raising young.

Many species found nowhere else in the world live from generation to generation in the ancient forests. In this way, these forests are like the ark.

Layers and Layers of Green

Ancient forests are rich in **species diversity**. Species diversity means that many different kinds of species survive in an area. There are several reasons why old-growth forests have so much species diversity. Climate and location are important. But even more important is the forests' **structure**.

Structure means the forest's shape, or the way it is put together. The structure of old-growth forests is a little like an apartment building. An apartment building is made of many floors. On each floor live a number of different people. Big families live in some apartments, while in others just one person may live.

The nests in the highest trees of the forest are like the top floor in an apartment building. The branches on very tall trees make layers and layers of green habitat for birds, animals, and even plants. Some plant species live their whole lives in the treetops! **Air plants** live on the broad branches of old trees. Certain

A silver fir tree provides different layers of habitat for animals and plants.

Spanish moss is an air plant that hangs from the branches of trees.

air plants coat the branches like a thick green carpet. Others hang and look like stringy green cotton candy. Air plants are food for some animals.

When a big tree dies and falls, it leaves a space in the forest where the sun's light can shine. In these spaces smaller plants grow, making food and shelter for more animals. Fallen logs are like the first floor in an apartment building. They provide a habitat for fungi, insects, plants, and animals.

If an apartment building is torn down, the structure of the building is destroyed. The people who lived there no longer have a home. It is the same when an ancient forest is cut down. The structure of the forest is destroyed. Plants and animals lose their habitat.

Extinction Is Forever

Some of the plants and animals that live in ancient forests cannot survive in any other place on earth. If one of these species loses its habitat, it will have no place to live and reproduce. Without a home, the species will die. When a species is gone forever from the earth, it is extinct.

If Noah's ark had sunk, all the species on board would have become extinct. The ancient forests are now like an ark with a hole in it. The old-growth forests are in great danger of losing the species that live within them. This is happening because the big trees are being cut down. If the cutting is not stopped, all the ancient forests will disappear. The ancient ark will have sunk.

The **extinction**, or death, of just one species can

When trees are cut down in an ancient forest, many animals and plants lose the habitat they need to survive.

affect the survival of other species, including humans. All living things are connected. They depend on each other for food, habitat, and reproduction. For example, many insects help plants reproduce by carrying pollen from males to females. Female plants can make seeds only after they receive pollen. Animals and birds also help plants reproduce by spreading the seeds. In fact, reproduction in many plants would not be possible without insects and animals.

The Web of Life

The way animals depend on each other, and on plants, for food is called a **food web**. A web is a group of paths that are all connected. A fishing net is a web because the strings cross over each other and are all connected. But if the net has a hole in it, it will not catch a fish. It is the same with a food web. If one part of the web is missing, the food web will not work.

One part of an ancient forest food web is made of owls that eat squirrels. The squirrels eat fungi that live in the ground. The fungi live off of the dead wood of old logs. Owls, squirrels, fungi, and trees depend on each other for life. If one of these species is removed from the forest, the food web will be destroyed.

Humans are living things, too. We need other living things in order to survive. Living things provide us with food and materials used by industries. We use different plant and animal species for medicines that cure diseases. One-fourth of all the medicines used in the United States come from plants. For example, the Pacific yew, a tree that grows in the ancient forests, is used to make a medicine that fights cancer.

Scientists have discovered and named no more

than 2 percent of the earth's species. There are at least 10 million and perhaps as many as 30 million left to find. Most of these species are plants and insects. Some are becoming extinct before we even have a name for them. We have learned to use some of the earth's species to help us live better lives. But we do not know the important benefits we can gain from plants and animals that have not yet been discovered. Every time a living thing becomes extinct, we might be losing something that could help us survive. Perhaps a medicine, a new food, or a new source of fuel is hidden in the ancient forests.

Even if humans could survive without species diversity, think what a boring world we would live in. Try to imagine the earth without all the different plants—grasses, flowers, and trees—of every size and color. Then try to imagine the world without tigers, elephants, zebras, penguins, and whales. Now try to imagine the earth without the birds and animals that live around your neighborhood or park. The world is beautiful because it is alive. And one part of the earth where amazing species live is the ancient forest.

The Pacific yew, as well as other trees and plants in ancient forests, could provide medicines that help fight deadly diseases such as cancer.

CHAPTER 4

A Circle of Life

▼

Hoo, hoo-hoo! Hoo, hoo-hoo! Hoo, hoo-hoo! The high-pitched hoot of the northern spotted owl sounds a little like the bark of a small dog. But few people have heard its hoot. And this owl is seen even less than it is heard.

The northern spotted owl lives high in the treetops of ancient forests. The spotted owl doesn't build its own nests. Instead, it uses large holes near the tops of old conifers. Sometimes spotted owls take over nests of other birds, such as hawks.

From its treetop nest, the spotted owl has a good view of the forest below. Its keen dark eyes can see a small wood rat, a red tree vole, and even a small flying squirrel. These animals are the owl's **prey**, its food. The owl is a **predator**, an animal that hunts and kills other animals for food. Spotted owls are good

A pair of spotted owls perch high on a tree branch in an old-growth forest.

nighttime hunters, and they catch their prey without making a sound.

Even though spotted owls are hunters, they are very tame around people. Usually they avoid human visitors to the ancient forests. But if you held a mouse in the palm of your hand, a spotted owl might swoop down and gently take it with its strong, hooked claws.

Spotted owls nest in pairs that stay together for life. Each spring the female owl lays two or three white eggs. The male brings food to the female while she sits on her eggs. After the eggs have hatched, the male owl continues to feed the mother and baby birds. In the fall the young birds begin to leave their nest and find new places to live in the forest.

The spotted owl's habitat is very large. Each pair of owls is spaced one to two miles apart so that the birds have enough food to hunt. Spotted owls can only live in old-growth forests.

Every day more and more of the spotted owl's habitat is cut down by loggers. As old-growth trees are lost, so are the owls. Now they are an **endangered species**.

An endangered species is one that is in danger of becoming extinct. Once a species is listed as en-dangered, the United States government must try to help save it. But time is running out. If too much old-growth forest is cut down, the spotted owl will become extinct because it will not have enough habitat.

Symbols of Wilderness

The spotted owl has become a symbol of ancient forests. Like the eagle, the American symbol of freedom, it is the symbol of the ancient wilderness. If the spotted owl can be protected, then the old-growth forests and other species that live there will also be preserved.

Other birds also need old-growth forests for their habitat. Brown creepers run up and down big tree trunks, looking for insects to eat. Vaux's swifts spend almost all their time flying—sometimes they fly for two or three years without stopping! They even eat insects in midflight. But they need to stop flying to nest and raise young birds. Vaux's swifts make their nests in snags that are common in ancient forests.

Beautiful and amazing creatures such as tailed frogs, Pacific giant salamanders, and banana slugs live near and in Westside streams. And some of the ancient forest **mammals** are among the most interesting in the world!

Mammals are a group of animals that give birth to live young and feed their babies milk from their mothers. Most have fur or hair on their bodies. Dogs, cats, elephants, whales, and humans are all mammals.

Voles are small mammals with thick fur and small eyes. Red-backed voles live in ancient forests. They dig

A red-backed vole eats mostly fungi.

burrows in the ground under rotting logs. The burrows are a safe place to live and raise their young.

Truffles and Trees

Red-backed voles are the only North American mammals that eat mostly fungi for food. The kind of fungi they live on are called truffles. Truffles grow under the ground and look like small potatoes.

Besides helping dead logs decompose, some fungi

also help living trees. Truffles live close to tree roots and help trees get more nutrients from the soil. Without truffles, conifers would not grow as strong or as tall as they do in the ancient forests.

Truffles are food for red-backed voles, and the voles help the fungi in an interesting way. Truffles contain spores that can grow into new truffles. When a vole eats a truffle, it is eating truffle spores that can live inside the vole's body. When the vole leaves behind its droppings, or waste, it is also leaving behind truffle spores.

These spores will some day grow into new truffles. In this way, voles also help trees grow. Voles spread truffles around the forest, and truffles help trees grow tall and strong. This is part of the food web in the ancient forest.

The northern flying squirrel is another small mammal that lives in old-growth forests. Its nests are in the holes of tall trees. Flying squirrels cannot really fly, but they glide downward from the treetops. They have loose folds of skin connecting their front and back legs. This skin opens like a parachute when the squirrel leaps into the air.

A flying squirrel prepares to leap from a tree.

Like the red-backed vole, flying squirrels eat truffles. And like the voles, the squirrels help trees grow by spreading truffle spores.

A Mansion in the Sky

Red tree voles also live in ancient forests. But they are very different from red-backed voles. They spend most of their lives high in the branches of Douglas firs.

The red tree vole builds its nest from Douglas fir

twigs and needles. But the nest is never really finished. It gets bigger and bigger as more and more families of voles live there. It grows from a small round house to a large "mansion" that wraps around the whole tree! Inside the mansion are many tunnels and mazes. There is always an escape tunnel that goes from deep within the nest to the bottom.

Red tree voles do not like to leave their comfortable nests. They sleep all day and come out at night to eat Douglas fir needles. They even get their water from the needles by licking off dew and rain.

Douglas firs can live to be many hundreds of years old. The nests of red tree voles can also be used for many hundreds of years. For generation after generation, families of red tree voles will live in the same tree. They will stay there until the tree dies and falls or until the tree is cut down by loggers.

We All Need Each Other

The amazing plants and animals that live in ancient forests are **interdependent**. Interdependence is the way species depend upon each other for survival. Some need each other for food. Others depend on a certain plant or animal to help them reproduce or for places to live.

Red-backed voles, red tree voles, flying squirrels, spotted owls, truffles, and Douglas firs all need each other to survive. They are species interdependent.

What would happen if any one of these species were taken away? All the other species would be affected. Some of them might even become extinct.

Today many species around the world are becoming extinct. Extinction is happening more now than during any other time in the history of the earth. Humans are causing species to disappear by destroying their habitats.

We do not yet know how extinctions of many species will affect us and our planet. But we do know that every time a species becomes extinct, the planet earth is less alive. The human race, like every other species, needs a living earth for life.

This is the meaning of the circle of life. All species are connected to make a circle. All species need other species for survival. The circle of life is another way of saying that living things are interdependent.

CHAPTER 5

A World of Good

▼

Ancient forests are complicated places. Here species live together and depend on each other for habitat, food, and for reproduction.

Scientists are just beginning to understand how humans need ancient forests. We depend on ancient forests for much more than places of beauty. Ancient forests are a valuable **natural resource**.

Natural resources are materials made by nature that people use. We use oil, coal, and natural gas for energy. **Timber** is also a valuable natural resource. It is the trees that are cut down and used for building and making wood products.

The timber in Westside ancient forests is the most valuable timber in the world because it is tall, strong, and old. Because of its great value, timber has been cut from ancient forests for more than one hundred years.

In an old-growth forest, a heavy truck hauls newly cut logs off to market.

If cutting continues, many scientists think that all the trees in the ancient forests will be gone by the year 2020. And along with the trees will disappear other valuable resources—resources that no amount of money can buy. The only way these resources can be saved is by stopping the cutting of old-growth trees.

In Sickness

The Pacific yew is one species of tree in ancient forests

that is not valuable for timber. Loggers usually burn these trees or let them rot. But in 1984 scientists discovered that Pacific yews are valuable for another reason.

The bark of the Pacific yew can be made into a powerful, cancer-fighting medicine called taxol. Cancer is a disease that spreads when cells in the body grow out of control. Taxol fights the spread of cancer by stopping wild cell growth.

Doctors need a lot of bark from the Pacific yew to make a small amount of taxol. But these trees grow very slowly, and now there are not enough of them left to make all the taxol needed.

About one in three Americans will suffer from cancer. Without strong medicines such as taxol, people with this deadly disease will have less chance of being cured. The only way we will have enough Pacific yews in the future is to protect our ancient forests now.

And in Health

Ancient forests also help protect the health of the earth. All living things, including people, need a healthy earth.

Ancient forests are like giant air filters that help clean the air we breathe. Trees take out some of the harmful things we put into the air. For example, trees are able to use some pollution from factories and cars as nutrients.

Trees also make **oxygen**. Humans—and almost all species—must have oxygen in order to survive. Oxygen is the part of air that keeps us alive. Without oxygen, a human will die within four minutes.

When we breathe out, we put **carbon dioxide** into the air. Carbon dioxide is an invisible gas that floats in the air. It is also put into the air when we burn fuels such as oil, coal, and wood. People are putting too much of this gas into the air. This is causing the **greenhouse effect**.

Have you ever been inside a greenhouse? It is a glass building that is used for growing plants. The sun shines into the greenhouse, making the air inside very warm.

The greenhouse effect happens when the sun's rays are trapped near the surface of the earth. The carbon dioxide in the air acts like a mirror. The mirror of carbon dioxide keeps reflecting the sun's rays back

The bark of the Pacific yew is used to make taxol, a cancer-fighting medicine.

to the earth. This causes the earth to get warmer. The heating up of the earth is called **global warming**.

If the temperature of the earth is raised too much, it could cause harm to living things, including humans. Ancient forests help slow global warming because trees take carbon dioxide out of the air. Less carbon dioxide in the air means that less sunlight will be trapped by the greenhouse effect.

But ancient forests alone cannot solve the problem of global warming. People must burn less fuel. This means driving our cars less, turning off lights, using less heating and air conditioning, and recycling our wastes.

Clean air is one part of a healthy earth, but we also need clean water. Our bodies are made mostly of water. Ancient forests help supply the earth with clean water.

The tops of tall trees reach into the clouds. Clouds are made of tiny water droplets. Water droplets stick to the needles on the trees and drip to the earth. The dripping water falls into the soil where trees can use it, or it falls into streams and helps keep them full during the dry summer. Streams flow into lakes that are used

Ancient forests help fill the streams
of the Pacific Northwest during dry summers.

by cities for drinking water. Without ancient forests, many cities in the Pacific Northwest would not have enough water during the summer.

Soil—Don't Treat It Like Dirt!

When heavy rains finally fall during the winter, the soil of ancient forests does not wash away. These giant trees have roots that hold the soil together. If an ancient forest is cut down, the rains will wash away the soil. This is called **erosion**. In these places no trees will grow because there is no fertile soil left.

Ancient forests also make soil. Huge trees that fall to the ground are broken down by fungi. Decomposing logs help make soil that is filled with nutrients, which are used again by growing trees.

Ancient forests are a priceless natural resource. They help build soils and prevent erosion. They clean the air, capture water from clouds, and help slow global warming. Old-growth forests are also home to many of species, which may help cure diseases.

Questions

Ancient forests remind us of a time when humans

were more connected with the earth. They help us remember that we are just one species on this planet. And ancient forests make us ask ourselves questions about our place in the world.

Is it our right to destroy other species? Is it our right to destroy a forest that took thousands of years to grow? Why are people cutting down the ancient forests? Once an ancient forest is cut down, can it be replanted by people? Who is to blame for the destruction? What can we do to save our ancient forests?

And Answers

Many Americans are surprised to learn that the ancient forests belong to them. All the old-growth forests that remain are found in America's national parks and national forests. Every citizen of the United States owns these parks and forests.

Trees cannot be cut down in national parks. These are places where animals and plants are protected. People visit national parks to hike, swim, camp, and enjoy being in a beautiful place. The ancient forests found in national parks are safe, but only three small national parks have ancient forests. Almost all of America's ancient forests are found in twelve of our national forests.

National forests are much different than national parks. They are places that are used for many things. People are allowed to hunt and fish in national forests. Because they can also be used for timber, the ancient forests are being cut down.

The United States government leases the national forests to logging companies. This means that logging companies must pay the government money so they can cut down trees. In other words, every American is selling old-growth trees to timber companies.

Why do we do this? To answer this question, we must first know the history of logging in the Westside.

A Way of Life

Logging started in the Westside in the 1820s. During the California gold rush of the late 1840s and 1850s, the logging business boomed. Throughout the 1900s, logging has increased every year. Now more than 85 percent of all the ancient forests have been cut down.

In the beginning, the trees in the best forests were

In 1905, a team of horses hauls an old-growth forest log with loggers on it in the Cascade Mountains.

logged first. Most were on private land owned by the timber companies. Because these forests were along rivers and streams, the trees were easy to cut down and transport.

In the early part of the 1900s, the timber companies did not plant any new trees after cutting down a forest. They just moved on to other forests and started logging again. This went on until the 1950s.

By that time the United States was growing

quickly. Thousands of houses were being built, and cities were growing. By 1960, the timber companies did not own any more old-growth forests. To stay in business, the companies turned to the national forests for places to cut old-growth timber.

Today the only old-growth forests left in the national forests are on mountainsides. They are much harder to reach. But since these trees are all that is left of old-growth forests, they are being cut.

When ancient forests are logged, every tree is taken. This is called **clear-cutting**. When a forest is cleared, habitat for many species is lost. The spotted owl has no place to nest, and the red tree vole has no Douglas fir needles to eat. There are no logs for fungi to feed on. The circle of life in the ancient forest is destroyed.

Clear-cutting also causes erosion. Since there are no trees to hold the soil together, rain washes the soil into streams. Fish cannot live in muddy water because their gills get clogged and they cannot get enough oxygen. Nutrients are washed away along with the soils.

But the logging continues because old-growth

The remaining ancient forests in the Westside national forests grow on mountainsides.

This aerial view shows the border between clear-cut private land and a wilderness area.

trees are very valuable. The trees are used for making houses, buildings, furniture, paper, and many other products. Cutting old-growth forests is the way many loggers earn a living. The loggers say they will lose their jobs if they are not allowed to cut down the ancient forests. To help the timber industry, the government keeps on leasing the national forests.

The End Is Near

If the cutting continues, the United States will have no remaining ancient forests. And the loggers will still lose their jobs, because there will no be trees left to cut. There are ways to save the forests and to help the loggers. The U.S. government could stop leasing the national forests and save the remaining ancient forests.

The government could help loggers by training them to do other jobs. In some Westside towns, logging has been a way of life for more than one hundred years. The government could help those towns start businesses that do not depend on logging.

The timber companies could also do their share. In the past, the logging companies did not do a good job of replanting the forests. Now they will have to wait about fifty years before they can cut down the new trees they have planted. In the future, the timber companies should plant forests that have more than one kind of tree in them. Like the ancient forests, forests with many species of trees also have more species of animals and other plants.

Once they are lost, the plants and animals of an ancient forest cannot be replaced.

Even though trees can be replanted, people cannot plant an ancient forest. It takes thousands of years for an ancient forest to grow. The plants and animals that live in ancient forests have lived on earth for millions of years. Once these plants and animals have become extinct, they can never be replaced.

The Future Is Now

The only way the ancient forests can be saved is if Americans get involved. Even those who are too young to vote can make a big difference. (See the Activity Pages on page 62 for ideas.)

It took millions of years for nature to create the ancient forests. In less than two hundred years from the time they were first logged, they could be totally destroyed. The future of the ancient forests is being decided now.

If we succeed in saving the ancient forests, we will be sending a clear message to people all over the world: "We care about our beautiful, ancient forests. We understand how we need our forests for a healthy earth. And we want the species of the ancient forests to live on into the future." Perhaps our message will help other people to preserve their ancient and magical places.

Here are some ideas to help save the ancient forests:

A. Talk to your parents, teachers, and friends about the ancient forests. Get people interested and involved. Try to learn more about the ancient forests and pass what you learn on to others.

B. Write letters to your U.S. senators and representatives. Tell them you want them to help save the ancient forests. Explain to them why it is important to save these forests. Tell them you are still young and that you think there should be species diversity, clean air, clean water, and beautiful forests left for you and your family to use and enjoy. Ask them to let you know about the actions they are taking to help save the ancient forests.

C. Get your school and community involved. One idea is to have a poster contest. Students can make posters about the ancient forests and why they are important. Have a local business donate a prize for the best poster.

D. Write letters to your local and national newspapers and magazines. Address each letter to the editor, and keep your letters short. Short letters have a better chance of getting published than long ones. Always sign your letters.

E. Use fewer products that are made from wood.Use cloth napkins and towels instead of paper ones. Use cloth bags for packing groceries instead of paper ones (ideas for making these are given on page 66). If there is a baby in your house, ask that your parents use cloth diapers instead of disposable ones. Millions of trees are used each year to make disposable diapers.

F. Use both sides of a piece of paper. And when you are finished with it, do not throw it out. Instead, save it, along with old newspapers, so it can be recycled. When something is recycled, it is used again. Paper can be recycled into new paper.

G. Use recycled paper products. Toilet paper, writing paper, computer paper, can be made from recycled paper.

H. Don't throw out things when they are broken. Try to fix them, or give them to someone who can. Every time something is thrown out it is replaced by new things that must be made. For example, fixing an old chair or table might save a tree from being used to make new furniture.

I. Learn about and join environmental groups that are working to save the ancient forests. Have a bake sale and use the money so your school class can join an environmental organization. The organization will send you information about the ancient forests and other issues affecting the earth. Ask your parents if your family could join an environmental group. Together decide which group your family is most interested in. (See page 67 for a list of environmental organizations.)

Chapter 1

1. <u>Look for conifers in your neighborhood or park.</u> Borrow a field guide about trees from the library, and bring it with you on your walk. Also bring a paper and pen and a bag. Look for as many different conifers as you can find. Try to identify them by using the field guide. Make a collection of pine cones and needles. Write down the names of the conifers you have discovered.

Chapter 2

2. <u>Go for a log hunt</u>. Look for old logs or stumps in your park or around your neighborhood. Look for fungi and insect tunnels on the surface of the log. If you can move the log, look underneath it and see if there are any insects or other animals. Gently dig a small sample of soil from under the log or next to the stump. Use a spoon to remove the soil and put it in a clean can. Return the log to its original place. Bring the soil home and use it for activity #8 (chapter 5).

Chapter 3

3. <u>Make a picture that shows the structure of an ancient forest</u>. Draw a poster (or use a chalkboard) of an ancient forest. Remember that an ancient forest is like an apartment building. Draw different animals and plants in the different layers of the forests. Look in chapter 4 for ideas about what animals to draw.

Chapter 4

4. <u>Make a food web.</u> Draw pictures of the plants and animals discussed in chapter 4. Cut the pictures out and put them on a bulletin board. Connect the species with yarn to show how the species are interdependent.

5. <u>Build a house of cards</u>. Draw pictures of the species that make up an ancient forest food web. Put each species on separate index cards. Now try to build a house using the cards. Once the house is built, pull out just one card. What happens to the house? What would happen to an ancient forest food web if one species is removed or becomes extinct?

Chapter 5

6. <u>Make your own soil.</u> In a pail collect some dirt, old

leaves, old grass clippings, and twigs. Try to find a couple of earthworms and put them in the pail. Gently mix the things in the pail and sprinkle some water on top. Keep the pail in a sunny window, and water it every few days. Keep track of how long it takes for the leaves, grass, and twigs to turn into soil.

7. <u>Find out what soil is made of.</u> To do this take an old jar with a lid. The jar should be the size of a large mayonnaise container. Fill the jar halfway with soil and fill the rest of it with water. Shake it up. Let it sit for a few days. Once the soil has settled you will see many layers in the jar. The biggest particles, like stones, have settled to the bottom to make the first layer. The second layer is sand. The third layer is called silt, which is composed of tiny pieces of rock. The fourth layer is clay. Clay is made of very fine particles. The top layer is humus. Humus is much lighter than the other layers because it is not made from rock. This is why it has "floated" to the top of the layers. Humus is made of the dead and decaying remains of plants and tiny animals. Fungi and other decomposers create humus.

8. <u>Find out what small animals live in soil.</u> Collect a sample in a clean can. (You can use the sample you collected in activity #2, in chapter 2.) Next, take a tall jar and put a funnel in the top of it. Put a piece of gauze inside the funnel. Empty the soil onto the gauze. Put the jar and funnel under a light and let it sit overnight. The light and heat from the lamp will cause the small animals to move through the gauze and into the jar. Try to identify the tiny animals you find the next morning.

9. <u>Make a natural water cycle.</u> You will need a terrarium,

which is a glass box or jar. You could use an old aquarium that is no longer used for fish. Or you could get a huge jar (check with a cafeteria or restaurant). In the bottom of the terrarium place soil from the woods. Next, plant several small plants. Moss and ferns work well. Make sure the plants you are using are common. Never remove rare plants from nature! Water the plants. Cover the terrarium with plastic wrap and poke a few small holes in the top. Why do water droplets form on the plastic wrap? Do you think you will have to water the plants again? How does this water cycle compare with the ancient forests?

10. <u>Make reusable grocery bags</u>. For this activity you will need these supplies: a spool of thread, scissors, pins, a sewing needle (or sewing machine), 1 and 2/3 yard (45 inches wide) OR 2/3 yard (60 inches wide) heavy canvas or denim material, 1 and 1/8 yard webbing material.

a. Cut a piece of material that measures 24 inches by 60 inches.

b. Fold the material (with right sides together) in half so it now measures 24 inches by 30 inches.

c. Pin the material together along each side.

d. Sew the material together along each side. When both sides are sewn together, sew it again for extra strength. (Try to use a sewing machine, because the bag will be much stronger.)

e. Now you have a bag, but the top edge is rough. Fold the top edge under and pin it to make a smooth edge.

f. Sew the top edge all the way around.

g. Make handles for the bag by cutting two pieces of

webbing. Each piece should be 20 inches long.

h. Measure 6 inches from each side of the bag and pin each end of the webbing pieces to either side of the bag at this place. Sew the webbing in place several times.

i. Now you have a shopping bag that can be used over and over. If you like, you can decorate this bag with fabric paints. Write an environmental message on your bag!

Environmental Organizations Working to Preserve the Ancient Forests

National Audubon Society
645 Pennsylvania Avenue, S.E.
Washington, D.C. 20003

Native Forest Council
P.O. Box 2171
Eugene, OR 97402

Sierra Club Legal Defense Fund, Inc.
2044 Fillmore Street
San Francisco, CA 94115

The Wilderness Society
1400 Eye Street, N.W.
Washington, D.C. 20005

Glossary

▼

air plants—plant species that spend their whole lives in tree tops.

carbon dioxide—the invisible gas found in the air that is a waste product from burning fuels such as wood, coal, oil, and gas. Living things also give off carbon dioxide as waste. Trees need carbon dioxide so they can grow.

clear-cutting—the way ancient forests are cut down. Every tree is taken, leaving nothing behind.

conifers—trees that have cones. Most conifers have needles that stay on the tree through the winter.

decompose—to rot or break down into smaller parts. Logs rot and are broken down into soil.

decomposers—living things that help things rot or break down. Fungi, bacteria, and some kinds of insects are decomposers.

endangered species—a species (group of plants or animals) that is in danger of becoming extinct; by law the United States government must work to protect species that are listed as endangered.

erosion—the washing away of soil by heavy rains. This happens when there are no tree roots or plants to hold the soil in place.

extinction—the death of a species. An extinct species is gone from the earth forever.

food web—the way plants, animals, and decomposers depend on each other for food.

fungi—a living thing that gets its food by decomposing the dead remains of other plants and animals.

global warming—the heating-up of the earth caused by the greenhouse effect. If global warming is not stopped, plants and animals may be damaged.

greenhouse effect—the trapping of the sun's rays near the surface of the earth by an invisible "mirror" of carbon dioxide and other gases. This causes the earth to become warmer. It is caused by pollution from cars and factories.

habitat—the area where a plant or animal naturally lives and the things it needs to survive (food, water, shelter).

interdependence—the way plants and animals need each other for life. Plants and animals can depend on each other for food, habitat, or reproduction.

log—a dead tree that has fallen to the ground. Logs are important to the forest because they help make soil. They are food for many insects and fungi. They are places for birds and animals to nest and find protection. And young trees begin life on old logs.

mammals—a group of animals that give birth to live young, feed their young mother's milk, and have hair or fur on their bodies.

natural resources—materials, such as coal, oil, gas, and timber, that are found on earth and that people can use.

nutrients—the parts of food that help plants and animals grow healthy and strong.

old-growth forest—an ancient forest; a forest that has reached the final stage of succession. Conifers are very tall. Smaller trees live below the big trees and can survive in the shade of these conifers. There are many snags and logs in such a forest.

oxygen—the invisible gas found in the air that many living things, including humans, must have for survival. Oxygen is made by trees.

predator—an animal that hunts and kills other animals for food.

preserve—to protect from danger; to save.

prey—an animal that is hunted, killed, and eaten for food.

reproduce—to make seeds, eggs, babies, or young. Some species breed or mate in order to make young.

snag—a dead tree that is still standing. Many birds and animals build nests in the tops of snags. Some birds use snags as lookouts.

species—a group of animals and plants that are alike in important ways. Plants or animals that belong to the same species can breed with each other and make seeds, eggs, or young.

species diversity—the millions of different kinds of plant and animal species on the earth.

spore—a small cell made by fungi that can grow into a new fungus.

structure—the way something is made or put together.

succession—the changes that happen over time in a forest or other natural area. The structure of the forest and the kinds of species that live in the forest change as the trees in the forest grow bigger. Fires, droughts, and diseases can cause succession to start again.

timber—the trees in a forest that are made into logs and used for building, making paper, or other wood products.

Index

▼